ARGENTINA: HUMAN RIGHTS

EXECUTIVE SUMMARY

Argentina is a federal constitutional republic. Cristina Fernandez de Kirchner won re-election to the presidency in October 2011 in multi-party elections the media and various nongovernmental organizations (NGOs) described as generally free and fair. The country also held legislative midterm elections on October 27. Security forces reported to civilian authorities but occasionally acted at lower levels independently of civilian control and committed human rights abuses.

The principal human rights problems included reports of torture by provincial police, harsh prison conditions, and gender violence.

Other human rights problems included use of excessive force by police; occasional arbitrary arrest and detention; prolonged pretrial detention; actions that risked impairing freedom of the press; continued concerns about judicial inefficiency; official corruption; child abuse; continuing discrimination against and infringements on the rights of indigenous people; sex trafficking; forced labor, primarily within the country; and child labor.

Judicial authorities prosecuted a number of officials who committed abuses during the year; however, some officials engaged in corruption or other abuses with impunity.

Section 1. Respect for the Integrity of the Person, Including Freedom from:

a. Arbitrary or Unlawful Deprivation of Life

There were reports of deaths as a result of the police's use of unwarranted or excessive force. Federal security forces have the authority to conduct internal investigations into alleged abuses and to fire individuals who have allegedly committed a human rights violation.

On September 30, two policemen from the metropolitan police and Buenos Aires province police force shot and killed a 29-year-old man after an argument. The security secretary asserted that one of the policemen intentionally fired his weapon, and remanded the case to the judge to investigate.

The NGO Coordinator Against Police Repression (CORREPI) reported in July that security forces using excessive force killed 56 persons during the first half of the year. The Center for Legal and Social Studies (CELS) reported deaths as a result of police using unwarranted or excessive force in the city of Buenos Aires and Buenos Aires Province during the first half of the year.

b. Disappearance

There were no reports of politically motivated disappearances.

Authorities continued to investigate and prosecute individuals implicated in disappearances, killings, and torture committed during the 1976-83 military dictatorship (widely referred to as the "Dirty War"). Investigations into the "systematic plan" of the military dictatorship, including the appropriation of children of detainees and the killing of detainees on "death flights," continued or began during the year. CELS estimated that 381 judicial investigations were active by May, in which 2,088 persons were charged for crimes against humanity. According to the Attorney General's Office for Follow-up on Crimes Against Humanity, from January to October the courts convicted 76 individuals for committing human rights abuses during the 1976-83 period and continued trials that were suspended in 1989-90 when the government issued a blanket pardon. For example, in September a criminal court of appeals upheld a conviction for the torture and murder of Carlos Moreno, a union representative and worker at the Loma Negra company. The tribunal sentenced three former army officials and two civilians to prison for their involvement in the case, ruling for the first time since these cases resumed that civilians had participated in crimes against humanity.

Judicial authorities continued to investigate cases of kidnapping and illegal adoption of children born to detained dissidents by members of the former military dictatorship. In April a judge sentenced a couple who illegally adopted the son of a disappeared family to six years in prison. The individual who illegally offered the baby to the couple also faced charges for identity theft. The NGO Abuelas de la Plaza de Mayo reported the number of persons illegally adopted by former military officials and later identified and made aware of their background increased to 109 of an estimated 500 born to detained and missing dissidents during the former military dictatorship.

The Argentine Forensic Anthropology Team (EAAF) continued cooperation with the government in the identification of remains of Dirty War victims. In August the National Institute of Industrial Technology (INTI) and the EAAF signed an agreement for INTI to provide technical support and assistance to the EAAF.

c. Torture and Other Cruel, Inhuman, or Degrading Treatment or Punishment

The law prohibits torture and other cruel, inhuman, or degrading treatment or punishment and provides penalties for torture similar to those for homicide. Nevertheless, international organizations, CELS, the Office of the National Public Prosecutor, and the Buenos Aires Provincial Memory Commission's Committee Against Torture (an autonomous office established by the provincial government) reported complaints of torture perpetrated by provincial and federal prison officials.

In September members of the Coordination and Follow-up System of Penitentiaries--a federal system with representatives from the Criminal Superior Tribunal, the General Prosecutor's Office, the National Defender's Office, the Federal Penitentiary, and CELS--visited various federal prisons. Their findings prompted the closure of some areas of Marcos Paz Penitentiary in Buenos Aires Province, where cells lacked electricity and bathrooms, and prisoners waited up to three months for access to shower facilities.

According to the 2012 annual report of the Buenos Aires Provincial Memory Commission's Committee Against Torture, deficiencies in food or health care and practices such as beatings, threats, and forced isolation remained common in prisons in the province of Buenos Aires. The report of the April 2012 prison visits of the UN special rapporteur on torture was not available by December.

Prison and Detention Center Conditions

Prison conditions often were harsh. Inmates in many facilities suffered from extreme overcrowding, poor nutrition, inadequate medical and psychological treatment, inadequate sanitation, limited family visits, and frequent degrading treatment, according to various reports by human rights organizations and research centers.

Physical Conditions: The number of prisoners in Buenos Aires provincial penitentiaries was approximately 30,000 and exceeded facility capacity by an estimated 92 percent, according to a 2010 report by the provincial Council of Defenders. Prison capacity in federal penitentiaries was adequate, according to the

Federal Penitentiary Service, with slightly more than 9,800 inmates in federal prisons and more than 10,900 beds.

Authorities held women separately from men, and the law permits children to stay in prison with their mothers until the age of four. According to the Federal Penitentiary Service, 785 women were in federal prisons. Women constituted 8 percent of the overall prison population. CELS estimated that 60 percent of the women incarcerated in Buenos Aires provincial prisons were in pretrial detention or awaiting sentencing, and many were held with convicted prisoners. In general men's prisons were more violent, dangerous, and crowded than women's prisons.

Overcrowding in juvenile facilities often resulted in minors being held in police station facilities, even though some NGOs and the national prison ombudsman warned the law prohibited doing so.

NGOs and media reports alleged poor prison conditions in several provinces. On April 14, a fire in a prison in the city of Rosario killed three prisoners and injured seven others. The lead prosecutor at the General Prosecutor's Office of Institutional Violence described current prison conditions as a "constant and massive violation of human rights" affecting 60,000 to 65,000 detainees.

Prisoners received potable water.

Administration: Information on the adequacy of recordkeeping and alternatives to sentencing for nonviolent offenders was unavailable. Prisoners and detainees generally had access to visitors and could observe their religious practices. Authorities permitted prisoners and detainees to submit complaints to judicial authorities without censorship and to request investigation of credible allegations of inhumane conditions. Some local NGOs noted, however, that access to a public defender was sometimes limited and that prisoners occasionally did not submit complaints to authorities due to fear of reprisal.

In August the national director of the Federal Penitentiary Service, Victor Hortel, resigned following complaints of alleged official complicity after 13 high-risk prisoners escaped from Ezeiza Penitentiary by digging a tunnel and breaking four boundary fences.

Independent Monitoring: The government permitted independent prison visits by local and international human rights observers, and such visits took place during the year.

d. Arbitrary Arrest or Detention

The law prohibits arbitrary arrest and detention, and the government generally observed these prohibitions; however, police reportedly arrested and detained citizens arbitrarily on occasion.

Role of the Police and Security Apparatus

The federal police normally have jurisdiction for maintaining law and order in the federal capital and for federal crimes in the provinces. Other federal police authorities include the airport security police, Gendarmerie, Coast Guard, and Bureau of Prisons. All federal police forces fall under the authority of the Security Ministry. Each province and the city of Buenos Aires also has its own police force that responds to a provincial (or city) security ministry or secretariat. Individual forces varied considerably in their effectiveness and respect for human rights. In late August, as a measure to combat growing insecurity, Security Minister Arturo Puricelli dispatched 5,000 additional Gendarmerie officers to assume urban policing duties in the province of Buenos Aires. In order to avoid leaving the borders unprotected, the army agreed to send soldiers to cooperate with the Gendarmerie in the border area with Brazil and Uruguay.

Federal security forces have the authority to conduct internal investigations into alleged abuses and to fire individuals who have allegedly committed a human rights violation. The federal government can also file complaints with the federal courts, and provincial governments can do the same for provincial security forces.

Members of security forces convicted of a crime were subject to stiff penalties. Generally authorities administratively suspended officers accused of wrongdoing until their investigations were completed. Authorities investigated and in some cases detained, prosecuted, and convicted the officers involved.

Arrest Procedures and Treatment of Detainees

Police generally apprehended individuals openly with warrants based on sufficient evidence and issued by a duly authorized official. Police may detain suspects for up to 10 hours without an arrest warrant if authorities have a well-founded belief that the suspects have committed or are about to commit a crime, or police are unable to determine the suspect's identity. Human rights groups reported police occasionally arrested persons arbitrarily and detained suspects longer than 10 hours.

The law provides a detainee with the right to a prompt determination of the legality of the detention by a lower criminal court judge, who determines whether to proceed with an investigation. In some cases there were delays in this process and in informing detainees of the charges against them.

The law provides for the right to bail except in cases involving narcotics, violent crimes, and firearms violations.

Authorities allowed detainees prompt access to counsel and provided public defenders in cases where they were unable to afford counsel. In some cases such access was delayed due to an overburdened system.

Pretrial Detention: The law provides for investigative detention of up to two years for indicted persons awaiting or undergoing trial; the period may be extended by one year in limited circumstances. The slow pace of the justice system often resulted in lengthy detentions beyond the period stipulated by law. According to statistics from the Federal Penitentiary Service, more than 5,400 detainees (of 9,800 prisoners) in federal prisons were in pretrial detention, awaiting sentencing, or awaiting the appeals process. According to several human rights organizations, 30 percent of pretrial detainees were eventually acquitted. A convicted prisoner usually receives credit for time already served.

e. Denial of Fair Public Trial

The law provides for the right to a fair trial, and the independent judiciary generally enforced this right. Judicial scholars continued to report inefficiencies and delays in the judicial system, and Chief Justice Lorenzetti asked criminal judges to speed up proceedings. According to some local NGOs, judges in some federal criminal and ordinary courts were subject occasionally to political manipulation.

Delays, procedural logjams, long gaps in the appointment of judges, inadequate administrative support, and general inefficiency hampered the judicial system. NGOs also criticized all three branches of the government for inefficiencies in the process for selecting judges. Judges' broad discretion on whether and how to pursue investigations contributed to a public perception that many decisions were arbitrary.

In May the National Congress approved a six-part presidential judicial reform project, including a Council of Magistrates reform law. In June the Supreme Court ruled four articles of the law unconstitutional, striking down a provision to select new judges by popular election, stating it disrupted the institution's balance of power and challenged judicial independence. In early May the UN special rapporteur on the independence of judges and lawyers expressed concern over parts of the project.

Trial Procedures

Trials are public. In federal and provincial courts, defendants enjoy a presumption of innocence and have the right to appeal, have legal counsel, and call defense witnesses. If needed, a public defender is provided at public expense when defendants face serious criminal charges. During the investigative stage, defendants can submit questions in writing to the investigating judge. A panel of judges decides guilt or innocence. Although defendants and their attorneys have access to government-held evidence, local NGOs indicated that defendants sometimes experienced obstacles or delays in obtaining such evidence. Defendants can present witnesses and provide expert witness reports, in addition to the defendant's own evidence. Lengthy delays in trials occurred nationwide, with many cases taking five or more years to resolve.

Federal and provincial courts continued the transition to trials with oral arguments in criminal cases, replacing the old system of written submissions. Although the 1994 constitution provides for trial by jury, implementing legislation was not passed by November. In Cordoba Province, however, defendants accused of certain serious crimes have the right to a trial by jury, and the province of Buenos Aires passed similar legislation in September.

An unofficially organized juvenile justice system operated in eight of 18 districts in Buenos Aires Province. It provides minors between the ages of 16 and 18 with the same procedural rights as adults and limits sentences to 180 days in prison.

Political Prisoners and Detainees

There were no reports of political prisoners or detainees.

Civil Judicial Procedures and Remedies

Citizens have access to the courts to bring lawsuits seeking damages or the protection of rights provided by the constitution. Local observers criticized various interested parties, including the government, for seeking to pressure judges and shape judicial outcomes to benefit the government.

Regional Human Rights Court Decisions

The country is subject to the jurisdiction of the Inter-American Court of Human Rights. In May the court ordered the country to reform the juvenile justice system to adhere to regional and international human rights conventions to avoid violating minor prisoners' human rights.

f. Arbitrary Interference with Privacy, Family, Home, or Correspondence

The constitution prohibits such actions, and the government generally respected these prohibitions.

In late April Cordoba Province police attempted without a warrant to evict 60 families squatting on vacantproperty.

Section 2. Respect for Civil Liberties, Including:

a. Freedom of Speech and Press

The constitution provides for freedom of speech and press; the government generally respected these rights. Independent newspapers, radio and television outlets, and internet sites were numerous and active, expressing a wide variety of views. Private media outlets were independent from the national and provincial governments.

Press Freedoms: All major supermarket and home appliance retailers ceased advertising in newspapers in February. Although retailers privately claimed the Domestic Trade Secretariat ordered this action to weaken independent media companies, no retailers publicly made this claim, which the government denied. While the limitation was in place, paid advertising decreased an estimated 70 percent, which organizations such as the Inter American Press Association (IAPA), the International Association of Broadcasting, and the Argentine Association of News Organizations cited as endangering press freedom through economic damage. The Consumers Union of Argentina launched a campaign protesting the ban on advertising. In July the government sanctioned the organization for misusing public funds to defend private media companies. Following changes in personnel at the federal level, including a new secretary of domestic commerce, there were indications near the end of the year that the restrictions had been lifted. In December many supermarkets resumed buying advertising in print and audiovisual news media.

Despite previous Supreme Court rulings ordering the government to apply reasonable balance in the distribution of public advertising, placement of official advertising remained arbitrary. In 2012 media outlets critical of the government received a disproportionately small fraction of the total public advertising budget. Official data showed that media groups close to the government obtained more than 45 percent of public advertising from 2009 to 2012. The two newspapers with the highest circulation and both critical of the government received less than 1 percent of the total public advertising budget. During the year the government agreed to abide by a 2009 federal appeals court ruling that withholding government advertising from Editorial Perfil outlets generally critical of the government violated freedom of the press as guaranteed in the constitution. As of October, however, the amount of public advertising in Editorial Perfil outlets was only between 7 percent and 16 percent of court-ordered levels.

The Supreme Court ruled in favor of the constitutionality of a media law passed in 2009 but still not fully implemented. On November 4, Clarin Group presented a voluntary divestment plan to comply with the law, which remained under government study in December.

Violence and Harassment: The Argentine Journalism Forum, an NGO promoting freedom of expression, reported 152 attacks on freedom of expression between January and September, up 32 percent from the same period in 2012.

On April 26, Buenos Aires city police agents attacked a group of 11 journalists and photographers from different media outlets who were covering a union protest at Borda mental health hospital. Police arrested one journalist and injured several others with rubber bullets. In reporting the Borda incident and two other capital city police attacks on journalists, CELs concluded that repeated attacks on journalists visibly carrying microphones or cameras in their hands seemed intended to prevent the recording and reporting of violent actions by police personnel.

On August18, following a television report by Clarin Group journalist Jorge Lanata on cases of alleged corruption, the secretary general of the presidency, Oscar Parrilli, issued a press release calling Lanata "a contract killer hired by

Magnetto" (Clarin Group's chief executive officer) and asserting his objective was to "spread hate" against President Cristina Kirchner. Parrilli subsequently added during a radio interview that Lanata was a "killer operating in the media." IAPA criticized those comments, warning they could trigger "more attacks against journalists."

<u>Censorship or Content Restrictions</u>: In August public television Channel 7 removed news anchor Juan Miceli from its daily news broadcast after an interview in which his questioning upset a ruling party congressperson. Other Channel 7 programs subsequently discredited Miceli, who was eventually dismissed.

Actions to Expand Press Freedom

The Supreme Court ruled in favor of a blogger being sued by a public university official for defamation, stating that opinions on the internet are protected by the same rights as those in traditional print or broadcast media. The court dismissed the case because the plaintiff was not able to prove actual malice. In another case the Civil and Commercial Court of Appeals ruled against a petition by a dental services company requesting Google to block negative comments against the organization.

Internet Freedom

There were no generalized restrictions on access to the internet or credible reports that the government monitored e-mail or internet chat rooms without appropriate legal authority. Individuals and groups could engage in the expression of views via the internet, including by e-mail and social networks. The International Telecommunication Union reported that 56 percent of individuals in the country used the internet during the year.

Academic Freedom and Cultural Events

There were no government restrictions on academic freedom or cultural events.

b. Freedom of Peaceful Assembly and Association

The constitution provides for freedom of assembly and association, and the government generally respected these rights.

c. Freedom of Religion

See the Department of State's *International Religious Freedom Report* at www.state.gov/j/drl/irf/rpt.

d. Freedom of Movement, Internally Displaced Persons, Protection of Refugees, and Stateless Persons

The constitution provides for freedom of internal movement, foreign travel, emigration, and repatriation, and the government generally respected these rights.

The government cooperated with the Office of the UN High Commissioner for Refugees (UNHCR) and other humanitarian organizations in providing protection and assistance to refugees, asylum seekers, and other persons of concern. According to the UNHCR, as of January there were 3,488 refugees and 1,921 asylum seekers residing in the country.

Protection of Refugees

Access to Asylum: Laws provide for the granting of refugee status, and the government has established a system for providing protection to refugees.

Statistics were not available on the number of individuals to whom the National Committee for Refugees granted refugee status, the number of asylum cases pending, or the total number of petitions filed during the year. Decisions on asylum petitions may take up to two years to adjudicate.

Section 3. Respect for Political Rights: The Right of Citizens to Change Their Government

The constitution provides citizens the right to change their government peacefully, and citizens exercised this right through periodic, free, and fair elections based on universal suffrage.

Elections and Political Participation

Recent Elections: In October 2011 voters re-elected President Cristina Fernandez de Kirchner of the Front for Victory coalition in polling described by media and various NGOs as free and fair. The country held legislative midterm elections on October 27. Voters elected one-half of the members of the Chamber of Deputies, representing all 23 provinces and the city of Buenos Aires, and one-third of those in the Senate, representing eight provinces. Local observers considered these elections generally free and fair.

Following 2012 legislation on voting rights, voters ages 16 and17 were added to the electoral register for the first time and participated in the August primary elections.

Participation of Women and Minorities: Regulations provide that at least one-third of the candidates on election slates for both houses of congress must be women. There were 28 women in the 72-seat Senate and 90 women in the 257-seat Chamber of Deputies. The president, two of the seven Supreme Court justices, and two cabinet ministers were women. (A third woman cabinet minister moved to a diplomatic post in May.) No known ethnic or racial minorities were in the national legislature. There were no known indigenous, ethnic, or racial minorities in the cabinet or on the Supreme Court.

Section 4. Corruption and Lack of Transparency in Government

The law provides criminal penalties for corruption by officials; however, multiple reports alleged that executive, legislative, and judicial officials engaged in corrupt practices with impunity, suggesting a failure to implement the law effectively.

Weak institutions and an often ineffective and politicized judicial system undermined systematic attempts to curb corruption.

Corruption: Cases of corruption occurred in some security forces. The most frequent abuses included extortion of, and protection for, those involved in drug trafficking and prostitution.

On September 3, a federal court in Cordoba Province imposed a six-month suspended sentence on former transportation secretary Ricardo Jaime for concealing documents connected with a judicial investigation for illicit enrichment. In June a judge in Misiones Province indicted police commissioner Hector Ojeda, the then head of the Investigations Unit in Iguazu Falls and one of Governor Closs' bodyguards, for alleged involvement in the robberies of supermarkets and a financial company. Ojeda was under investigation for allegedly covering up the activities of drug traffickers and criminals in the tri-border area.

Allegations of corruption in provincial as well as in federal courts remained frequent.

Vice President Amado Boudou remained under investigation for illicit enrichment and for using his former position as minister of economy to benefit the Old Fund Company, a firm in which he had a financial interest. Although Federal Judge Ariel Lijo rejected Boudou's request to throw out the case in August, Cassation Court Judge Javier De Luca ruled in November that courts must immediately assess the evidence in order to continue the case. Additionally Federal Judge Norberto Oyarbide was investigating Boudou in connection with funds that disappeared during Boudou's administration of the country's social security administration.

On June 14, a court convicted former president Carlos Menem and former defense minister Oscar Camilion of arms smuggling to Ecuador and Croatia and sentenced them to five to seven years' imprisonment. Menem also was indicted for his alleged responsibility in the 1995 explosion in a military factory in Rio Tercero, Cordoba Province, which resulted in seven deaths and 300 persons injured. As a senator, Menem holds immunity.

The case charging that former president Fernando de la Rua and senior members of his cabinet bribed national senators in 2000 to vote for the amendment of a labor law continued at year's end.

Whistleblower Protection: Criminal code provisions oblige public officials to file complaints if they witness irregularities. Public employment laws protect officials from termination of employment in such cases but do not cover other forms of retaliation. Cases of corruption can be anonymously reported to the Anticorruption Office of the Ministry of Justice and Human Rights.

Financial Disclosure: Public officials are subject to financial disclosure laws, and the Ministry of Justice's Anti-Corruption Office (ACO) is responsible for analyzing and investigating federal executive branch officials based on their financial disclosure forms. Laws provide for public disclosure, but not all agencies complied, and enforcement remained a problem, since authorities did not sanction public officials for noncompliance. The ACO is also responsible for investigating corruption within the federal executive branch or in matters involving federal funds, except for funds transferred to the provinces. As part of the executive branch, the ACO does not have authority to prosecute cases independently, but it can refer cases to other agencies or serve as the plaintiff and request a judge to initiate a case.

Public Access to Information: While the country does not have a law that provides for public access to government information, a presidential decree provides for access to public documents and information that fall within the jurisdiction of the executive. In August the Supreme Court ordered judges' affidavits to be posted on the Supreme Court's website. A September report by a local NGO reported continuing arbitrary rejections of requests for information, allegedly violating the Habeas Data Law, which specifically provides public access to judicial records and reports of judges' personal assets.

Section 5. Governmental Attitude Regarding International and Nongovernmental Investigation of Alleged Violations of Human Rights

A wide variety of domestic and international human rights groups generally operated without government restriction, investigating and publishing their findings on human rights cases. Government officials usually were cooperative and generally responsive to their views.

Government Human Rights Bodies: The government has a Human Rights Secretariat. Its main objective is to collaborate with the Ministry of Justice, Security and Human rights to promote policies, plans, and programs for the protection of human rights. During the year it published leaflets and books on a range of human rights topics.

In June Prosecutor General Alejandra Gils-Carbo inaugurated the Office of Crimes Against Humanity, charged with investigating and documenting human rights violations that occurred under the military dictatorship of 1976-83.

In July the Ministry of Economy and Public Finance created the Commission for Memory, Truth and Justice to compile information about the workers of the ministry who were persecuted, detained, kidnapped, disappeared, or killed during the military dictatorship.

Section 6. Discrimination, Societal Abuses, and Trafficking in Persons

The law prohibits discrimination based on race, gender, sexual orientation, disability, language, or social status, and the government generally enforced these prohibitions.

Women

Rape and Domestic Violence: Rape, including spousal rape, is a crime, but evidentiary requirements, either in the form of clear physical injury or the testimony of a witness, often presented difficulties in prosecuting such crimes. The penalties for rape range from six months' to 20 years' imprisonment. There were no reports of police or judicial reluctance to act on rape cases; however, women's rights advocates claimed that attitudes of police, hospitals, and courts toward survivors of sexual violence sometimes revictimized the individual.

No statistics were available on the number of rape cases reported during the year. Many rapes went unreported due to fear of further violence, retribution, and social stigma.

The law prohibits domestic violence, including spousal abuse, and complaints are addressed in civil courts to secure protection measures. Family court judges have the right to bar a perpetrator from a victim's home or workplace. The law requires the state to open a criminal investigation potentially resulting in life imprisonment in cases where violence results in death. In November 2012 Congress passed the Femicide Law, imposing stricter penalties on those who kill their spouses, partners, or children as a consequence of gender violence. In July the executive branch enacted a law creating a national DNA registry of sex criminals. According to local NGOs, lack of police and judicial vigilance often led to a lack of protection for victims.

Domestic violence against women was a problem. The civil society organization La Casa del Encuentro reported that 209 women died between January and September as a result of domestic or gender-based violence. Approximately half of these cases occurred in the provinces of Buenos Aires, Cordoba, and Santa Fe. Of these killings, 68 percent involved a husband, boyfriend, or former boyfriend. In at least 20 cases, the woman had filed a complaint against the aggressor for domestic violence.

The Supreme Court's Office of Domestic Violence provided around-the-clock protection and resources to victims of domestic violence. The office received approximately 830 cases of domestic violence each month in the city of Buenos Aires, an estimated 64 percent of which involved violence against women. The office also carried out risk assessments necessary to obtain a restraining order. The "Victims against Violence Program," which operated in the city of Buenos Aires and Chaco Province, empowers a team of specialists from the Justice and Security Ministry to assist victims of domestic violence. The program reported an average of 700 telephone calls per month.

Since 2008 there have been 1,236 reported cases of femicide. Since the highly publicized murder of Wanda Taddei, who was burned to death by her husband in 2010, there have been 66 similar killings, including seven in the first half of the year.

The Ministry of Social Development of the province of Buenos Aires reported 221 formal complaints of physical abuse against women during the first three months of the year. Individuals ages 20 to30 constituted a majority of the victims, and 53 percent of the cases involved psychological and emotional mistreatment.

Pursuant to an October 2012 agreement, the Office of Domestic Violence and the Security Ministry trained members of the Federal Police, Navy, and Gendarmerie in the city of Buenos Aires on domestic violence intervention. Statistics on the number trained were not available at the end of the year.

Public and private institutions offered prevention programs and provided support and treatment for abused women. The Buenos Aires Municipal Government operated a small shelter for battered women.

Sexual Harassment: The law prohibits sexual harassment in the public sector and imposes disciplinary or corrective measures. In some jurisdictions, such as Buenos Aires City, sexual harassment may lead to the abuser's dismissal, whereas in others, such as Santa Fe Province, the maximum penalty is five days in prison.

Reproductive Rights: Couples and individuals generally had the right to decide freely the number, spacing, and timing of children and had the information and means to do so free from discrimination, coercion, and violence. Access to information on contraception and skilled attendance at delivery and in postpartum care were widely available. The law requires the government to provide free contraceptives, and an estimated 64 to70 percent of women used modern contraceptive means.

Discrimination: Although women enjoyed equal rights under the law, including property rights, they continued to face economic discrimination and held a disproportionately high number of lower-paying jobs. Women also held significantly fewer executive positions in the private sector than men, according to several studies. Although equal payment for equal work is constitutionally mandated, the 2013 Global Gender Gap Report estimated that women earned approximately 58 percent as much as men for similar or equal work.

The Supreme Court's Office of Women trains judges, secretaries, and clerks to deal with court cases related to women's issues; it also seeks to ensure equal access for women to positions in the court system. The office also trained judges, prosecutors, judicial staff, and law enforcement agents to increase awareness of gender-related crimes and develop techniques to deal with gender-related cases and victims.

Children

Birth Registration: The country provided universal birth registration, and citizenship was derived both by birth within the country's territory and from one's parents. Parents have 40 days to register births, and the state has an additional 20 days to do so. The Ministry of Interior may issue birth certificates to children under age 12 whose births were not previously registered.

Child Abuse: Child abuse was common; for example, the Office of Domestic Violence reported that 30 percent of the cases it received per month involved children.

Forced and Early Marriage: The legal minimum age of marriage for men and women is 18.

Sexual Exploitation of Children: Sexual exploitation of children, including in prostitution, was a problem. The minimum age of consensual sex is 18. There is a statutory rape law with penalties ranging from six months to 15 years in prison, depending on the age of the victim. Additionally, regardless of age, if a judge finds evidence of deception, violence, threats, abuse of authority, or any other form of intimidation or coercion resulting in sexual intercourse, the minimum sentence increases to six years. Several prominent cases of child sexual abuse were reported during the year. During the first half of the year, the Ministry of Justice program Victims against Violence assisted 329 minors who were victims of sexual abuse.

The law prohibits the production and distribution of child pornography with penalties ranging from six months to four years in prison. While the law does not prohibit the possession of child pornography by individuals for personal use, it provides penalties ranging from four months to two years in prison for possession of child pornography with the intent to distribute it. Additionally the law provides penalties ranging from one month to three years in prison for facilitating access to pornographic shows or materials to minors under the age of 14.

During the year prosecutors and police pursued cases of internet child pornography. In August Federal Police arrested 30 individuals for producing and distributing child pornography online. They discovered 1,500 CDs, computers, and external disks with pornographic material.

On July 30, authorities in Cordoba arrested a teacher for distributing child pornography online, charging him with distribution and commercialization of child pornography. After conviction, a court sentenced the individual to two years' imprisonment.

International Child Abductions: The country is a party to the 1980 Hague Convention on the Civil Aspects of International Child Abduction. For information see the Department of State's report on compliance at http://travel.state.gov/abduction/resources/congressreport/congressreport_4308.html as well as country-specific information at http://travel.state.gov/abduction/country/country_5875.html.

Anti-Semitism

The Jewish community consisted of approximately 250,000 persons. Sporadic acts of anti-Semitic discrimination and vandalism continued. The Delegation of Argentine Jewish Associations (DAIA) received complaints of anti-Semitism during the year.

The most commonly reported anti-Semitic incidents were virtual slurs posted on various websites, graffiti, verbal slurs, and the desecration of Jewish cemeteries. In 2012 the DAIA received 243 distinct reports of anti-Semitic behavior. The city of Buenos Aires had the most cases filed, and the DAIA claimed cases in the provinces were likely underreported. On March 19, the municipality of General Campos, Entre Rios Province, distributed tax-payment receipts printed with the sentence: "Be a patriot, kill a Jew." The DAIA declared that municipal authorities were responsible for the bill and demanded administrative sanctions and removal from office of the responsible party.

The investigation continued into the 1994 bombing of the Argentina Israelite Mutual Association (AMIA) community center in Buenos Aires that killed 85 persons. The federal prosecutor investigating the case continued to seek the arrest of eight Iranians for their alleged involvement in the bombing. Early in the year the government ratified a memorandum of understanding with Iran to jointly investigate the AMIA case, and the government continued to negotiate with Iran on the specifics of the agreement's implementation. Jewish community representatives and opposition political leaders continued to criticize the government for engaging in an unclearly conditioned political dialogue and expressed concerns that it could undermine the country's existing judicial investigation. Jewish organizations AMIA and DAIA filed suit against the agreement in July, arguing that the accord is unconstitutional.

The Buenos Aires City government partnered with the interfaith organization Bridge Builders and the French Alliance to sponsor a series of monthly film presentations and discussions to promote religious understanding.

Trafficking in Persons

See the Department of State's *Trafficking in Persons Report* at www.state.gov/j/tip.

Persons with Disabilities

The constitution and laws prohibit discrimination against persons with physical, sensory, intellectual, and mental disabilities in employment, education, air travel and other transportation, access to health care, or the provision of other state services. A specific law also mandates access to buildings by persons with disabilities. While the federal government has protective laws, many provinces have not adopted the laws and have no mechanisms to ensure enforcement. An employment quota law reserves 4 percent of federal government jobs for persons with disabilities, but NGOs and advocacy groups claimed the quota often was not respected.

According to the Ministry of Labor, Employment, and Social Security, more than 12,000 persons with disabilities had obtained jobs through the ministry's programs in the city of Buenos Aires as of May 2011. The programs included various benefits for workers with disabilities, such as free job training programs.

A pattern of inadequate facilities and poor conditions continued in some mental institutions. For example, a press report from April addressed deficient infrastructure and human rights violations in Buen Pastor Psychiatric Hospital in Bell Ville, Cordoba Province. The report described prisoners living in "concentration camp" conditions with open sewers infested with insects and bats' nests in kitchen facilities. Governor De la Sota committed to improving services through increased financial support and advocated to end confinement practices for patients with less severe disabilities.

In early February, following a 2012 request from more than 30 NGOs, the Buenos Aires City education ministry issued regulations to allow children with disabilities to attend schools with their therapists and health-care companions. The effort aimed to promote the inclusion of children with disabilities in schools that also admit children without disabilities. In October three NGOs submitted a report to the UN Committee on the Rights of Persons with Disabilities, sharing concern over discrepancies between domestic legislation and international conventions that guarantee rights to persons with disabilities. The NGOs also claimed Argentina was falling short of compliance with the UN committee's 2012 recommendations to the country.

In August and October, official voting centers for primary and legislative mid-term elections provided special voting tables and braille ballot holders, making the voting process accessible to persons with disabilities.

The National Advisory Committee for the Integration of People with Disabilities under the National Council for Coordination of Social Policies has formal responsibility for actions to accommodate persons with disabilities. The government's actions to improve respect for the rights of persons with disabilities included a program started in September 2012 by Buenos Aires Province that establishes economic incentives for municipalities that hire persons with disabilities as civil servants. The program stipulated that municipalities participating in the program would receive a subsidy payment from the provincial Ministry of Labor.

Indigenous People

The constitution recognizes the ethnic and cultural identities of indigenous people and states that congress shall protect their right to bilingual education, recognize their communities and the communal ownership of their ancestral lands, and allow for their participation in the management of their natural resources. Indigenous people did not fully participate in the management of their lands or natural resources, in part because responsibility for implementing the law is delegated to the 23 provinces, only 11 of which have constitutions recognizing indigenous rights.

Although there is no formal process to recognize indigenous tribes or determine who is an indigenous person, indigenous communities can register with the provincial or federal government as civic associations. A 2010 survey conducted by the National Statistics and Census Institute recorded an indigenous population of more than780,000.

During his visit to the country in late 2011, the UN special rapporteur on the rights of indigenous people, James Anaya, found the "historical exclusion of indigenous peoples is still very apparent," manifested by "the inadequate protection of their rights to their traditional lands, and their continuing marginalization and discrimination." Poverty rates were higher than average in areas with large indigenous populations. Indigenous people had greater than average rates of illiteracy, chronic disease, and unemployment. Indigenous women faced further discrimination based on gender and reduced economic status. The lack of trained teachers hampered government efforts to offer bilingual education opportunities to indigenous people.

The special rapporteur's report indicated indigenous peoples continued to lack adequate participation in decisions affecting their ancestral lands. It added that projects carried out by the agricultural and extractive industries displaced individuals, limited their access to traditional means of livelihood, reduced the area of lands on which they depended, and caused pollution that in some cases endangered the health and welfare of indigenous communities. Local NGOs agreed these findings remained valid during the year.

In May the president of the Social Care Pastoral Committee of the Catholic Church, Bishop Jorge Lozano, expressed concern over the marginalization of indigenous populations throughout the country as exemplified by rates of extreme poverty, illiteracy, and illness. His concerns focused on the Qom community in Formosa Province, and he placed responsibility on the federal and provincial governments.

In May policemen killed a Toba community member in Chaco Province after a violent eviction. Representatives of the Qom Community blamed the Chaco vice governor, Juan Carlos Bacileff Ivanoff, who allegedly ordered the eviction.

Additionally, Abelardo Diaz, son of Qom chief Felix Diaz, was the victim of a violent attack by a group of 30 individuals. Other members of Diaz' family suffered systematic attacks during the year, which local analysts and NGOs attributed to Diaz' repeated demands for formal ownership of Qom land. Formosa provincial authorities minimized the importance of the attacks.

A land survey, initiated by the federal government in 2011, continued during the year. Various NGOs, national deputies, and the Catholic Church claimed the National Institute for Indigenous Rights, the entity charged with surveying land, had mapped only 12 percent of the entire territory despite funding sufficient to make greater progress.

Societal Abuses, Discrimination, and Acts of Violence Based on Sexual Orientation and Gender Identity

Lesbian, gay, bisexual, and transgender organizations operated freely. They worked closely with academic institutions, NGOs, and government authorities without interference.

There was no official discrimination based on sexual orientation in employment, housing, statelessness, or access to education or health care. Overt societal discrimination generally was uncommon, but the National Institute Against Discrimination, Xenophobia, and Racism reported cases of discrimination and police brutality toward the transgender community. In August a transsexual prisoner at Ezeiza Penitentiary reported serious mistreatment by prisoners and penitentiary officials, which two witnesses later confirmed. After the witnesses provided their testimonies, prison guards injured them and confined them to isolation and a psychiatric area.

In April Pedro Robledo was the victim of a violent hate crime at a university party in Buenos Aires. Robledo met with the university president and petitioned for the amendment of the antidiscrimination law to include an article on sexual minorities.

Other Societal Violence or Discrimination

There were no known reports of societal violence against persons with HIV/AIDs, but there were occasional reports of discrimination against persons with the disease. For example, the president of the Argentine Network for People with AIDS reported obstacles for infected individuals to obtain employment. According to the president, medical checkups that diagnose the disease prevent approximately 60 to78 percent of individuals from being hired.

Section 7. Worker Rights

a. Freedom of Association and the Right to Collective Bargaining

With some restrictions, the law provides for the right of all workers to form and join "free and democratic labor unions, recognized by inscription in a special register," conduct legal strikes, and bargain collectively. The law prohibits military and law enforcement personnel from forming and joining unions. The law prohibits discrimination against unions and protects workers from dismissal, suspension, and changes in labor conditions. The law provides for reinstatement for workers fired for union activity.

The law allows unions to register without prior authorization, and registered trade union organizations may engage in certain activities to represent their members, including petitioning the government and employers. The law grants official trade union status to only one union deemed the "most representative" per industrial sector within a specific geographical region. Only unions with such official recognition receive trade union immunity for their officials, are permitted to deduct union dues directly, and may bargain collectively with recourse to conciliation and arbitration. The most representative union bargains on behalf of all workers, and collective agreements cover both union members and nonmembers in the sector. The law requires the Ministry of Labor, Employment, and Social Security to ratify collective bargaining agreements.

The Argentine Workers Central (CTA) and other labor groups not affiliated with the General Confederation of Labor continued to contend that the legal recognition of only one union per sector conflicted with international standards and prevented these unions from obtaining full legal standing. In June the Supreme Court decided a case reaffirming the need for more than one official union per sector and for amendments to the legislation. Congress had not modified labor legislation, however, and the executive branch had not granted such recognition to the CTA by the end of November.

Civil servants and workers in essential services may strike only after a compulsory 15-day conciliation process, and they are subject to the condition that unspecified "minimum services" be rendered. Once the conciliation term expires, civil servants and workers in essential services must give five days' notice to the administrative authority and the public agency that they intend to strike. If "minimum services" were not previously defined in a collective bargaining agreement, all parties then negotiate which minimum services will continue to be provided and a schedule for their provision. The public agency, in turn, must provide clients two days' notice of the impending strike.

The government effectively enforced these laws. Under the law complaints for unfair labor practices can be brought before the judiciary. They may result in a fine being imposed on the employer, or the relevant employers' association where appropriate. There were few cases of significant delays or appeals in the collective bargaining process.

Workers exercised freedom of association and employers respected the right to collectively bargain and to strike. Labor organizations operated independently of government and political parties.

b. Prohibition of Forced or Compulsory Labor

The law prohibits all forms of forced or compulsory labor, and the government generally enforced such laws. Penalties for violations range from four to 15 years in prison and are comparable to other serious offenses. The Ministry of Security and the National Program of Rescue and Accompaniment of Victims under the Ministry of Justice and Human Rights reported rescuing 284 potential victims of forced labor from January through June. The labor ministry carried out several inspections during the year and found various irregularities and potential cases of forced labor. Holding perpetrators accountable and providing victims with services continued to be a problem.

Forced labor occurred. Employers subjected a significant number of Bolivians, Paraguayans, and Peruvians, as well as Argentine citizens from poorer northern provinces, to forced labor in sweatshops, agriculture, and domestic work. Men, women, and children (see section 7.c.) were all victims of forced labor, although victims' gender and age varied by employment sector.

In June the Airport Security Police detained a Colombian citizen on charges of leading an international forced-labor network. The police identified more than 202 Colombians recruited through misleading job offers who were potential victims of forced labor.

In September police agents arrested 10 individuals allegedly participating in an international labor-trafficking network. The network offered attractive jobs in Argentina to Chinese citizens, who travelled to Buenos Aires via Paraguay.

Traffickers sold the victims to Chinese supermarkets, where they worked more than 12 hours a day in deplorable conditions.

Also see the Department of State's *Trafficking in Persons Report* at www.state.gov/j/tip.

c. Prohibition of Child Labor and Minimum Age for Employment

The minimum age for employment is 16. In rare cases labor authorities may authorize a younger child to work as part of a family unit. Children between the ages of 16 and 18 may work in a limited number of job categories and for limited hours if they have completed compulsory schooling, which normally ends at age 18. Children under 18 cannot be hired to perform perilous, arduous, or unhealthy jobs. The law requires employers to provide adequate care for workers' children during work hours to discourage child labor.

Provincial governments and the city government of Buenos Aires are responsible for labor law enforcement. Legal penalties for employing underage workers range from 1,000 to 5,000 pesos ($200 to $1,000) for each child employed. Subsequent violations may lead the labor authority to close the company for up to 10 days, and the company is then prevented from becoming a vendor to the government for a year. On March 20, the Senate unanimously passed a law punishing child labor with penalties ranging from one to four years' imprisonment, unless the crime falls under a more serious category. The law excludes parents. These penalties are sufficient to deter violations.

While the government enforced applicable laws, observers noted that inspectors often were well connected to the subjects of inspection and that corruption remained an obstacle to compliance, especially in the provinces.

Child labor occurred. According to a 2004 government survey, an estimated 450,000 children worked, amounting to 7 percent of children between the ages of five and 13 and 20 percent of children over the age of 14. Employing preliminary data from the corresponding 2012 survey, the Ministry of Labor reported a 66 percent decline in child labor rates between 2004 and 2012. In rural areas children worked on family and third-party farms producing such goods as blueberries, cotton, garlic, grapes, olives, strawberries, tobacco, tomatoes, and yerba mate. Children working in the agriculture sector often handled pesticides without proper protection. In urban areas some children engaged in domestic service and worked on the street selling goods, shining shoes, and recycling trash. According to government sources, some children worked in the manufacturing sector producing such goods as bricks, matches, fireworks, and garments. Children also worked in the mining, fishing, and construction sectors. Officials noted reports of children forced to work as street vendors and beggars in the capital. Commercial sexual exploitation of children occurred as well (see section 6, Children).

Also see the Department of Labor's *Findings on the Worst Forms of Child Labor* at www.dol.gov/ilab/programs/ocft/tda.htm.

d. Acceptable Conditions of Work

In August the government increased the monthly minimum wage for most workers to 3,300 pesos ($660). The National Census and Statistics Institute estimated a family of four needed 1,708 pesos ($342) to remain above the poverty line.

Federal law sets standards in the areas of health, safety, and hours. The maximum workday is eight hours, and the maximum workweek is 48 hours. Overtime pay is required for hours worked in excess of these limits. The law sets minimums for periods of rest, requiring a minimum of 12 hours of rest prior to the start of a new workday. Sundays are holidays, and those required to work on Sundays are paid double. Labor law mandates a minimum of 14 days and a maximum of 35 days of paid vacation, depending on the length of the worker's service.

The law sets premium pay for overtime, adding an extra 50 percent of the hourly rate on ordinary days and 100 percent on Saturday afternoons, Sundays, and holidays. Employees cannot be forced to work overtime unless work stoppage would risk or cause injury, the need for overtime is caused by an act of God, or other exceptional reasons affecting the national economy or "unusual and unpredictable situations" affecting businesses occur.

The law requires employers to insure their employees against accidents at the workplace and when traveling to and from work. The law requires that employers either provide insurance through a labor risk insurance entity or provide its own insurance to employees to meet specified requirements set forth by the national insurance regulator. In October 2012 Congress amended the Labor Risks Law to increase compensation for workers' death or incapacity, while limiting the workers' entitlement to file a complaint if the workers accept the insurance company's compensation.

In March Congress unanimously approved an amendment to the domestic employee law that expands workers' rights and benefits to domestic employees, rural workers, freelance workers, and the volunteer firemen corps.

Laws governing acceptable conditions of work were not enforced universally, particularly for workers in the informal sector. The Ministry of Labor, Education, and Social Security has responsibility for enforcing legislation related to working conditions. The ministry continued inspections to ensure companies registered their informal workers. During the year the government increased labor inspections to detect unregistered or compulsory work, mainly in rural areas. During 2011, the most recent year for which data are available, the Labor Ministry reported that it had 479 labor inspectors. Information was unavailable regarding the number of inspections during the year, violations encountered by inspectors, and fines or penalties imposed. According to a 2007 study by the International Labor Organization, 60 percent of employed citizens ages 15 to 24 were engaged in informal labor. The Superintendence of Labor Risks serves as the enforcement agency to monitor compliance of health and safety laws and the activities of the labor risk insurance companies.

Most workers in the formal sector earned significantly more than the minimum wage. In general the minimum wage served to mark the minimum pay an informal worker should get, although formal workers' pay was usually higher.

According to the Labor Risk Superintendency, in 2010, the most recent year for which data were available, there were 61.6 worker fatalities per million workers. Agriculture recorded 184.6 fatalities per million workers, construction 196.7 fatalities per million, and transport 157.2 fatalities per million.